DUNGENESS CRAB
Metacarcinus magister

RIVER OTTER
Lontra canadensis

A GEODUCK IS NOT A DUCK

A STORY OF A UNIQUE PACIFIC NORTHWEST MOLLUSK

Candy Wellins   Illustrated by Ellie Peterson

little bigfoot

an imprint of sasquatch books
seattle, wa

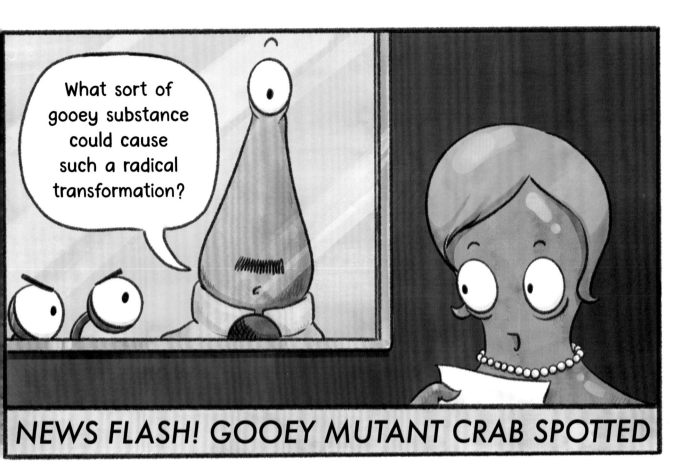

NEWS FLASH! GOOEY MUTANT CRAB SPOTTED

...PARENTS, KEEP YOUR KIDS HOME! MUTA

...REST IN PEACE GOOEY

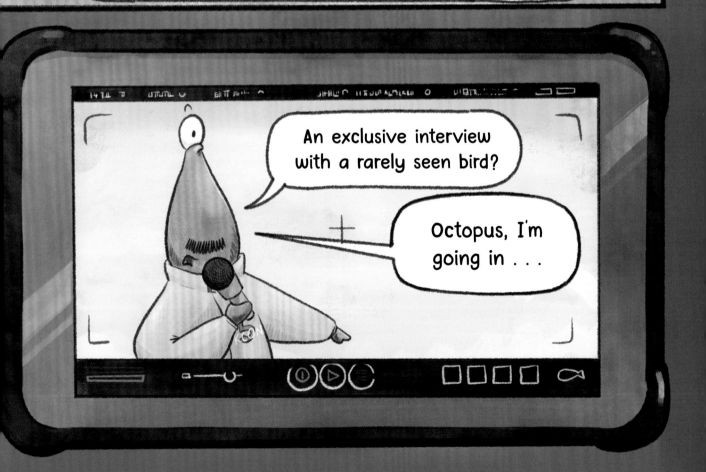

ONGOING *SITUATION*: GOOIER GOOEY DUCK BELOW

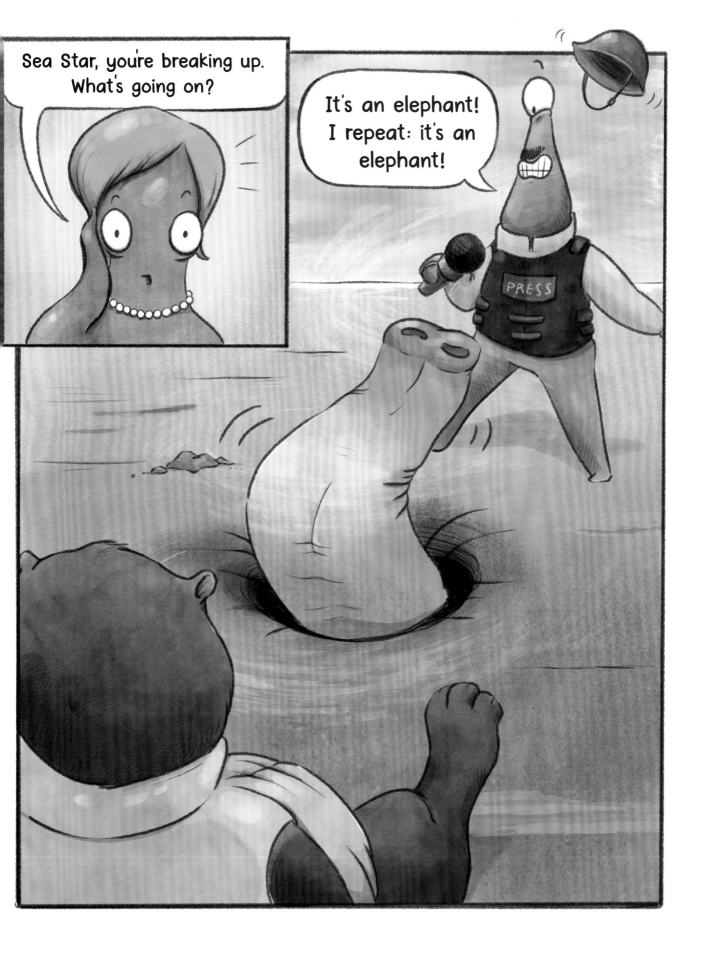

And thanks to your investigative digging, you exposed him.

THE TRUTH ABOUT GEODUCKS

Geoducks are neither gooey nor ducks. They are the largest species of burrowing clams in the world. They are found on the Pacific coast of the United States and Canada, from Washington State through British Columbia and into Alaska.

The geoduck name is derived from the Nisqually word gʷídəq, which means "dig deep." Because a geoduck's body is much longer than its shell, geoducks are vulnerable to predators (like crabs) and bury themselves deep in the sand for safety.

A geoduck's body is composed of a long, double-barreled siphon attached to a much smaller shell. Picture an elephant's trunk with two round nostrils at the end. One side sucks up water and the other side spits it out. A geoduck's siphon may be over three feet long while its shell is rarely longer than eight inches.

Though their shells do little to protect them, they do have one useful purpose. Each year of its life, a geoduck adds a ring around its shell (much like the annual rings on the inside of a tree's trunk). Geoducks who manage to evade predators can live very long lives. Geoducks are one of the longest-living animals on earth and frequently live more than one hundred years.

And yes, elephants are herbivores and do not eat ducks or geoducks.

You can learn even more about geoducks by visiting this website:

SeattleAquarium.org/blog/all-about-geoducks

For Brian who may have needed convincing that
geoducks were real, but has always believed in me. —CW

For my brother David, and all the fun we had
while mom hunted geoducks. —EP

Manufactured in China by C&C Offset Printing Co. Ltd. Shenzhen,
Guangdong Province, in September 2023

LITTLE BIGFOOT with colophon is a registered trademark
of Penguin Random House LLC

28 27 26 25 24   9 8 7 6 5 4 3 2 1

Editor: Christy Cox | Production editor: Peggy Gannon
Designer: Anna Goldstein | Interior photograph: © ucko/AdobeStock

Library of Congress Cataloging-in-Publication
Data is available.

ISBN: 978-1-63217-397-3

Sasquatch Books
1325 Fourth Avenue, Suite 1025
Seattle, WA 98101

SasquatchBooks.com

CANDY WELLINS was born and raised in the Pacific Northwest where she spent many days chasing after geoducks. She now lives in Texas with her husband and three children and spends her days chasing down ideas for new picture books. You can find out more about her at CandyWellins.com.

ELLIE PETERSON is a picture book author and illustrator who loves combing beaches for delectable mollusks and wishes she could have an otter for a pet. She lives in the Seattle area with her family and her dog, Daisy. You can find out more about her at ElliePetersonArt.com.